PUTTING THE PIECES TOGETHER

Sharon Whitehill

Fernwood
PRESS

Putting the Pieces Together

@2025 by Sharon Whitehill

Fernwood Press
Newberg, Oregon
www.fernwoodpress.com

Printed in the United States of America

Cover and page design: Mareesa Fawver Moss
Cover art: Tatiana Tochilova

ISBN 978-1-59498-161-6

*To my three precious daughters, to my heart-and-soul sister
and near-sister cousin, to my grandson and granddaughter,
to her little one, and to all their own families in turn.*

How I love you all.

Special mention for Kurt and Rick.

Contents

I. *Family Puzzles*

Seeing Stars

A house built on sand makes itself felt when a mother
hides glasses of whiskey in the drawers of her vanity table.
That our family was special and blessed was the wishful
fiction read to us children at bedtime. *Asteroid and disaster
are linguistic siblings;* the Milky Way is a road of milk, a spill
of cream in a black-coffee heaven; *and* stars, though regarded
as gods by the Greeks, are merely dense balls of gas that spewed
their chemical guts into the galaxy. "Let the stars sit where they will,"
Coyote cries in the Navajo myth, flinging up handfuls of glittering
mica that stick to the sky helter-skelter. My flame-haired mother
saw shades of gray that my father was blind to, yet she projected
her own tortured colors on each of us in turn, her afternoon empathy
sucking me in to be spat upon later. Etymologies tell more truth
about life than the words do themselves, as in *the Greek prefix sark
linking sarcasm to sarcophagus, literal eater of flesh. Like my mother,
a* star in its red giant phase, devouring her innermost planets, the milk
of her human kindness curdled by accusations that *ripped me apart
like hyenas tearing the flesh from my bones.* A star-crossed ancestral
curse hounded *my* Janus-faced mother, who winked out at last
like a star.

The Intimate Room

My grandmother bathed with her underwear on
and undressed every night in the closet,
guarding the intimate room of the body
she'd dutifully given in marriage.

Her daughter, my mother,
derided her mother's Puritan shame
but imprisoned herself in an alternate room,
alcohol's padded cell.

Which liberated her tongue
to a pornographic and savage excess
that helped to wall up her self-doubt
and fortified her enough
to feint at seducing a family friend.
Also the man who delivered the laundry.
And even the officer
summoned one night to the park
where she'd fled in her nightgown
and hurled herself down on the ground.

Unlike my grandmother's closet,
my own intimate room
is spacious enough for two.
It is neither a hideout nor prison
but a room sacrosanct
in the house I have built.
No chink for the ghosts
of the two damaged women I loved.

Mildred Remembers Her Mother Mae

Mae did what she could to improve me,
put my hair up in rags every night
to make ringlets, topped with a big floppy bow.
Which only convinced me how homely I was
with my big bumpy nose
and the all-over freckles I couldn't erase
with complexion creams, skin bleach,
or the "mercolized wax" that promised
to peel them off gently.

And no way to compete with my brother,
so black-haired and tall,
or vie for the smiles she beamed on him
after frowning on me.
Nowhere to turn except my little dog Jackie
and the affectionate cat I tried to keep safe
by tying it up to the porch,
never forgiving myself when it strangled.
Resentment and grief soon converted
into the rage that drove my attack on those boys
I saw drowning kittens down at the creek.

I learned to look down on her, my mother,
note her indifference to my intellectual gifts,
her prudish avoidance of sexual talk,
her devotion to the same God
who damned unchristened babies to hell
and made nakedness shameful.
To defy her, I painted my lips,
bobbed my hair, rolled my waistbands
to shorten my skirts.

An intestinal fortitude that deserted me
after my first escape from the place
and this woman I hoped to transcend:
my own weakness made plain when I crept back,
overwhelmed, from the state teachers college.
Too fragile again ten years later
to cope with working and living alone in the city,
ministered to by the gentleman friend
who made me his unfulfilled wife.

Major breakdowns, these,
where I honed the skill of deflecting the focus
away from my weakness and into my bitter contempt
for those I needed the most.
Including my mother,
unpardoned still for diminishing me—
this my bone-deep belief—
by elevating my brother: a boy, a man,
equally flawed and equally, visibly,
lacking in grit.

Yet how could I not need her, too,
for being mother so resolute?
Who shouldered her widowhood like an Atlas,
weathered the death of that one cherished son,
took over the care of his child?
How could I fail to call out for her
from the bed where I lie dying:
Help me, help me, Mama.

Rites of Passage

A child pushed and squeezed through
a cleft cut into a sapling. Boys who endure,
without crying, stinging ants inside their gloves.
Girls who dance without rest for four days.
But no such ordeal to mark my own coming of age,
the transitional moments distinctive only
in being anticlimactic. "Pomp and Circumstance"
finished playing before I reached the stage;
first sex exciting as Instant Wheat Ralston;
university alienating enough to abandon
in favor of marriage and moving away.
Each traditional symbol less a commencement
than a slow leakage of essence of self.

Until my first child was flopped on my belly,
squirming and wet, and a flood of love
that lifted me up like a wave and poured out
of my eyes: mind, body, and heart coalesced
in a single great starburst of joy. A peak experience,
yes, a transformation profound as it was unexpected.
In Joseph Campbell's less grandiose words,
You have been thinking one way,
and you now have to think in a new way.

A second transformative moment, years later,
the death of my mother Mildred: not a surprise
yet a shock that left me feeling exposed
as a crab after shedding its shell, stripped
of the buffer that stood between me
and the next generation to die. Nothing to do
except follow my feet where they walked
through the night streets of London, hours

as fittingly barren as my childbirth memories
were rich. Isolated, alone, I felt only the tide
going out and out. A long-period wave
and only the curve of debris on the beach
to mark its return.

Apex Predators

The wolf whistle first, then the slap on the bottom
that left my skin burning under the thick winter coat.
How much do you cost? the man called. Orcas are
known as the wolves of the sea, having recently damaged
the rudders of dozens of vessels. Not really attacks,
experts say, just playful behavior. In first grade,
a gang of boys held me down in a ditch, pushed my face
in the mud: as if I'd been wearing a sign that said *Kick Me.*
Which later changed to *Kiss Me* but meant the same thing:
a male neighbor pressing me into a full-body hug
in the grocery store aisle. "What did you do to entice him?"
other shoppers seemed to be thinking at me. The question
pierced like a dart. Apex predators, orcas. The triangular dorsal fin
of the male juts six feet high. Half-jealous, my girlfriends
made jokes: *Men swarm you like flies on honey.* Or on rotting meat,
I thought as I turned from a drink at the fountain to find
several guys waiting, their own thirst postponed by their hunger
for me. *Oh please, not again!* cried the skipper whose boat
had been sunk once before. *They knew what they wanted this time.*
They bit off both rudders and didn't touch anything else.
A chiropractor to whom I never returned cracked my spine
while standing behind me. I felt his erection. The Etruscan god
of the underworld, Orcus, who gave orcas the name, punished
breakers of oaths. A man I knew punished his broken lawnmower
by shooting it with a .22. Later we laughed at the story, but now
I don't know why we found it funny. Running home to my mother
after the beating, I felt my teeth scrape grains of dirt.

Unpeaceable Kingdom

Sweet white wallpaper lambs
gaze down on the barely grown girl,

a pillow pulled over her ears
to muffle the roar of the lioness

who paces outside her locked door.
A mother sweetly maternal in daylight

transformed at night to a maenad
determined to strip and to shred.

A father, born under Leo himself,
no match for a Sphinx in her wrath,

a Sekhmet rampaging for blood.
No hope but to wait out the frenzy,

count on the fuel that provoked it
to put her to sleep.

Photographs

When a spring snowstorm turned the world white
on the day of a wedding, the light from the windows
illumined a guest with flamingo-pink hair. A wavelength
of color, a beautiful hue, that emerged in the photos
as garish hot pink, seducing the eye of the viewer
away from the bride. In some pictures of me with my children,
I have paper-punched my face out, each perforation the ghost
of an unlovely likeness, leaving a scatter of Os in the album,
a series of *moms* with no vowel. On my first wedding day,
a freak snowstorm with thunder and lightning: weird
weather, we joked, that must be a sign from the gods.
Perception is fickle. In my forties and fifties, I harangued myself
as not slim enough and already grown old, whereas what I see now
in photos of me are dark brows on the wing above eyes
the rich brown of a newly turned field and lips, then despised
as too thin, fulsome with laughter and speech. The yellow O
of the sun in drawings of children belies its true color, white,
as revealed in the prismatic light of the rainbow. A mirrored reflection,
however pleasing, is of the moment, while photos make permanent
every unflattering angle and grimace. No color at all at my wedding,
only a black-and-white snapshot of us as we stood,
he trim in his Air Force blues, I in my too-tight dark dress,
on the sidewalk in front of that Midwestern courthouse,
before the storm.

The Sisters Corner

for Roxy

Today in one coffee-shop alcove,
a pair of young women have claimed
the ochre-print loveseat and table,
rerouting me to the opposite nook
with a duplicate loveseat and table
to wait for my sister.
Ensconced with my latte,
I glance across the room
at the women who've taken our favorite spot.

One in profile to me
seems to be telling a story,
the other is wearing a pink baseball cap
and listening with her whole body:
a mutual focus that hooks my attention
in spite of the tables between us
and surly habitué John partly blocking my view.
The surge of identification I feel
undermined by a question:
how long will it be before the rapt listener
is permitted to speak in her turn?
Or, as so frequently happens in pairs,
will the talk pouring out on one side
inhibit what might billow up on the other?

I look away, sip my latte,
consider the give and take of conversation
that moves with the rhythm and flow of a dance.

I love women! is my predicable thought,
as I turn back to witness the moment
these two trade roles without breaking their gaze:
the pink-capped former listener
now alight with her own eager tale,
the raconteur listening, engrossed.

A mirror image of us on that loveseat.

On impulse I rise, cross over to them,
they turn to me, smiling, surprised,
and I see in their features a further resemblance:
they are sisters, too.

In a Family Way

My granddaughter Isla tried to say *Grandma*
when she was a child, a word that emerged as *Bambi*:
I wonder what names her child will later bestow
on my daughter and me. In Canada, six generations
in an unbroken line of women took monikers different
enough that the kids could distinguish each grandma
from all the others. In some whale species, the females
cease in midlife to bear offspring but, like humans,
live decades longer to share in the nurture of their line
of descendants. Having achieved great-grandmother
status myself, I'm now privileged to witness one more
genetic edition of Me—a reflection, perhaps, of the truth
that what's separate from us is also *of* us. Whale
young develop signature whistles that set them apart,
the way my grandniece's voice could reach air-horn levels,
the way Fanny Brice garnered "Baby Snooks" radio fame
with her little-girl pitch. Humpbacks "converse"
in units of sound—whups, barks, and growls—combined
into phrases with a reliable syntax; sperm whale clans
create codas of clicks that identify each by the dialect
of its ocean locale. Sameness in difference. A vernacular
as distinct as my own family argot: phrases borrowed
from Shakespeare and Monty Python.

II. *Missing Pieces*

Missing Pieces

Surely a mythical creature, the starfish: what looks like
a skullcap crawling along the sea floor on its lips,
with nary a torso or tail. Osiris's wicked brother
chops his body to pieces and scatters the parts in the Nile—
a transgression peculiarly heinous when afterlife access requires
that even a god be physically whole. Losing a piece, a starfish
regrows the appendage; from that one lost arm an entire
new creature sometimes evolves. Absent such cellular magic,
the loss of human parts can be what *permits* the renewal,
as in surgeries to save my daughters: one with breast cancer,
the other with uterine tumors. Isis collects every piece of Osiris
except for his phallus, consumed by a fish—what better way
to convey the fall of a fertility god? Some female starfish flirt
with a form of dismemberment, splitting in half to become
a male pair who turn female again when mature. The illusion
of safety, so vital to human function and purpose, is easily shaken.
Late at night, when I'm waiting alone after the airport has emptied,
my husband appears at last like an angelic vision: a resurrection,
of sorts, of our life together. Isis reassembles her husband,
fully equipped through her magic, embalms him, wraps his body
in linen—thereafter the rites that reanimate dead Egyptians
as mummies. In my own life, no mythical sorcery or echinoderm
alchemy to restore a lost limb, a disappeared loved one, a self.
Rather, only postponement, the holding of loss in abeyance.
Which seems to me magic enough.

Almost Bionic

Biology is destiny. —Sigmund Freud

I believe I have outsmarted Freud:

a bounteous bosom replaced
by small silicone gummies
that free me from binding brassieres,
gleefully burned in a barrel,
which balances out the subtraction
of maternal mechanics below.

Later, hard plastic and batteries
aided amplification
of hammer, anvil, and stirrup,
while metal and polyethylene
supplanted a hip's ball and socket.

Today acrylic resin and metal
sit where a tooth used to be,
intraocular plastic lenses
replace the real things.

Repaired, reattached, and rebuilt:
artificial in part although functional still.
A destiny Freud was unable to see
in his wildest dreams.

Late Grace

After Gerard Manley Hopkins

Praise be to my ears for their recent auricular ease:
Apprehending the sizzle of rain, like damp logs in a fire;
The whoosh-whistle of wings as the mourning dove flies;
The cat's interrogative chirp; whispers that tickle and tease;
Clipped-consonant plosives, the crackle of sparks on a wire;
And all susurration, its hums and murmurs and sighs.

All that rustles, rumbles, chuckles, or skirls;
Whatever is mellow, melodic—one voice or a choir—
In pitch, pulse, timbre, tone. Each rediscovered surprise
An easeful companion, returned from afar: sound and sight
                    Harmonized.

No Power in a Square

Human beings prefer gentle curves—the acorn's
plump cup, a horse's double-globed haunch—
over the points of a crystal or pyramid,
perhaps because the first contours babies perceive
are the curves of a face, the warmth of encircling arms.
As even the straightest observable line can never
be perfectly straight in the structures we build,
so curvature dominates nature: from massive
planets and suns gravitationally sucked into spheres
to galaxies spread into wide-ranging discs.

Sounds, too, assume curvilinear shapes: a chanted OM
graphs on the cymascope as an ellipse,
as if imitating the orbits of planets and moons;
other devotional mantras emerge as intricate figures
that look like mandalas. Once, when I witnessed
a murmuration of starlings in Denmark, the thrum
of thousands of wingbeats struck me
as onomatopoeia embodied: a vast curtain of bends,
waves, and curls poised second by second to tip
and transform; every quicksilver switch dependent
on each bird's fine-tuned response to a shift
in its seven nearest neighbors.

Long ago, Black Elk asserted that "Everything tries
to be round," a personification of the ubiquitous urge
that causes the whirlwind to spiral, the sky and horizon
to arch like a bowl, and his people to honor the wisdom
of birds ("for theirs is the same religion as ours") in a circle
of teepees they saw as their nest full of nests.
A culture of curves, lost to the little square houses
where they ended their days.

A Tumor Made of Teeth Found in
the Pelvis of an Ancient Egyptian

In a multi-chambered underground tomb,
a young woman of 18 or 20, a calcified clump
in the cup of her pelvis. Not a fetus,
as archaeologists thought, but a teratoma:
one embryonic germ cell gone rogue,
multiplied into a tumorous mass presenting as teeth,
a growth made of dentin, enamel, cementum.

For the first time ever I think about teeth
vis-à-vis their location. I remember the boy
who flung *You're a buck-toothed jerk!* at me
when I was ten, after which four years of braces
and the white smile that still gleams
from the pages of my high school yearbook.
At times I still dream of spitting them out,
one by one, in my hand.

Teratoma, from the Greek *teras*, meaning monster.
This discovery in Egypt is rare, a tumor
of tissue so hard it lasts thousands of years:
a single tumor that split over time into another tooth
nestled on top of the young woman's leg bone.
Two molariform pieces complete in themselves,
an enamel crown each, with its own roots.

I think about teeth and recoil at the image of molars
transplanted below and within. See myself
as a young woman of twenty, *Pregnancy, Birth,*
& Family Planning splayed on my chest,
eyes closed to visualize arm buds and leg buds,
fingernails, eyelashes, growing and growing.
Never tumors of teeth.

A young woman, placed in the tomb
with her hand curved on her pelvis,
a body arranged as if to mirror
how someone clutches herself at the source of the pain
or communes with what grows in her womb.
On one finger, a ring with an image of Bes,
protector of mothers and children: a fertility god
garbed for battle, ithyphallic, aroused.

I think about teeth as symbols: of maturity, beauty,
or health. About mine, still intact after decades,
still respectful of their jurisdiction.

Burning Mouth Syndrome

Lips that prickle and sting
to the point that it's painful to speak:
sore, chapped, and peeling
along their vermillion border.
Perhaps an allergic reaction
to tomatoes, potatoes, eggplants, peppers,
all staple foods in my usual diet,
all nightshades,
and all now forbidden.

Atropa belladonna, deadly nightshade,
named for the beautiful lady, Atropos,
who cuts the life-thread with her shears.

My own destiny, too,
seems doomed to be severed—
not from my physical life
but from those moments each night
when I long to savor my favorite cuisines
as I listlessly swallow steamed chicken and rice

and yield to the fantasy
that I've somehow slighted the Family Nightshade
by plucking their cousin, the mandrake,
while weeding my garden:
a fatal act, according to folklore,
that condemns me to hell.

This as likely a reason for the inferno
raging around the contours of my lips
as that my own body would turn against me,
sentencing me to a flavorless fate.

Litmus in the Lunchbox

Their friends at school pretended to gag
as my girls ate sandwiches of sliced beef tongue,
a mild-flavored meat delicious with mustard
or pepper and salt. Though we laugh today,
my children and I, at how closed-minded
the neighbors where they grew up, I remember
my own refusal to sample a chocolate-dipped cricket,
how I still look away as my daughter savors fish eyeballs.
A delicacy, she points out, in multiple cultures
outside the West.

Protein is protein, yes, a fine mantra.
Even when it's pronounced by someone (myself)
who is no more exempt from such insular bias
than those small-town kids
who favored their peanut butter and jelly.
Witness also my uneasy memories of Iceland,
my unfeigned revulsion at rotting shark meat,
fermented ram testes, and roasted sheep's heads.

Why should the pork sausage I eat with my eggs
or the tongue I once sliced for our lunches
feel so remarkably different from the head of a sheep
with its ears, eyes, and tongue on my plate?
Why does the very idea of eating a face
seem so much more disgusting than the minced
mix of its various parts?

Perhaps it has something to do with
those smiley-faced M&Ms that didn't sell
or the reluctance to bite off the head
of a gingerbread man. Something to do,
in the case of the pig or the sheep,
with confronting the truth that I'm eating
a creature that once was alive.

Tongues in Trees

And this our life, exempt from public haunt,
Find tongues in trees, books in the running brooks. —As You Like It

Long before *Goodnight Moon* was composed,
I said hello every night to my pillow, my lamp,
and my woolly orange blanket: a cozy reunion
after the long day apart with companions alive
and as connected to me as the family cats. An outlook
my parents indulged, dissipating as I grew up,
a human habit of mind that sees each living
and non-living thing as a being, a self.

A lost gift, Wordsworth opined, which he equated
with memories of heaven that fade as we age,
though according to Freud it's merely an immature
cultural stage superseded by reason and science.
Not so different, to me, from the woman
who thrilled to the image of Jesus, burned like a brand
on the tortilla she scooped from her griddle.
Nor unlike those wee faerie folk in green scarves,
light dancing around them, acknowledged not only
by Scottish villagers but by the Galloway doctor
who hid from them on the dark road as they trooped past.

Perhaps we too easily dismiss them as pagan perceptions,
these everyday objects and places imbued with mysterious magic.
Like Mauna Kea, the mountain revered as the eldest
of ancestor gods in Hawaii. Like Taranis, thunder deity
of Roman Celts but also the thunder itself. Like spirits
who live inside the masks of the Bwa people of Mali
and Burkina Faso.

Projection, psychologists say: ideas and feelings
imprinted on concrete locales. And yet they survive:
in the storm hag of Scotland who washes her tartan
until it turns white and falls as the snow; in the divinities
of the tribal Malaysian Semang, who dwell in stone pillars
and under the earth; in sacred Navajo beings like Ma'ii,
the coyote, Nilch'i, the wind, or alien gods like the Monster
Who Kicks People Down Cliffs.

And even the otherwise secular person who once
had a vision of all things in nature as one:
every tree, leaf, blade of grass, he said, lit from within
as if incandescent. Such moments, most often granted
to mystics and very young children, serve others,
serve me, as a humbling reminder of how small we are
in the vast network of being.

Danse de l'arboriste

A hurricane-blasted live oak,
a convoy of trucks lined up on the road,
the Bobcats and crane standing by
along with a crew
of woodchippers, trimmers, and drivers.
It could be a stage,
ensemble in place,
the principal dancer in harness and helmet.

He anchors himself to the tree,
tosses his lanyard over a branch
with the ease of an angler casting for trout,
clips it to a rope attached to the crane,
and chainsaws the limb
until it breaks free of the trunk
to be lifted away by the crane
and eased to the ground.

There the ensemble awaits:
trimmers to barber the branches,
Bobcats to bare their black teeth,
clamp them on each fallen limb
and carry it off to the trucks
to be chipped into mulch
or split into firewood.

No swans rising out of a lake. Instead,
fog of chainsaw exhaust and cut wood
as the dancer reprises each move
in a limb-by-limb sequence
of looping, securing, clipping, and sawing
set to an orchestral soundtrack that features
the *brum-brum-brum-brrrrrr* of the saw,
the crack of a branch breaking free,
and the rumble of Bobcats below.

A performance as choreographed
as Gene Kelly's dance in the rain.
A Baryshnikov of the trees.

On the Dance Floor with Glass

This is the puzzle of glass:
it's a substance that at the molecular level
is neither a liquid nor solid but halfway between.

Liquid molecules
        cha-cha around each other
                like sassy dancers
                        in ruffled dresses and sleeves.

Whereas, in solids, they sit
out the dances
in orderly rows.

Yet in glass they're a fluid melange,
        crowding the dance floor
but locked in place
        as if enchanted mid-glide:
liquid dancers arrayed
        in their now-stiffened gowns.

Such an anomaly, glass: a contradiction
in chemistry, as well as in terms:
an "amorphous (non-crystalline) solid"
that debuts a new form of matter.

Mind the Stairs

Those flagstone steps to the darkened backyard
which, ever after, carried the stigma of being the place
where my high school boyfriend came in my hand;
and the carpeted staircase, bones creaking with age,
that turned traitor to me as I sneaked in.

The ladder, bolted into a rock, that led up
to the ancient cliff dwellings: I gamely climbed it
with everyone else and failed to account
for the backward-facing descent—until I froze there,
one foot groping for purchase in empty air.

The staircase in our old farmhouse, that stopped
at the second-floor wall: no landing, only a doorway
to one side, the hall to the other, and nothing to do
but turn right or turn left. Less amusing, the open-rise
stair steps into the demi-world of the cellar.

And now these terraced steps I wend my way down
to a place surrounded by fan palms, beauty berry,
coontie, ferns, and a slow-moving river below,
thence to a patio made of memorial pavers,
one of them bearing my husband's name.

Here I will read aloud the letter I wrote him
an hour ago, sit for a while on a bench, then burn the letter
and save the cooled ash for my drawer of mementos.
A ritual marking this day for as long as I'm able
to manage the stairs.

Loving the Questions

Nobody knows how a lump of gray matter
engenders a mind that's aware of itself.
How consciousness fishes images
out of the depths as we sleep—a bay horse
with a white blaze, the long-ago slur of a bully—
messages in an old bottle washed up on the beach.
No one knows what equips the brain
to fashion an alphabet, compose a sonata,
decipher the structure of DNA.
I don't understand why my neighbor
sets fireworks off in his driveway,
why the frangipani outside my window
grows branches each year but no flowers,
or why your dear body surrendered its life
while my own marches on.
Though I carry you with me like home.

And still, here's the world:
the bright sky above me,
the music of chimes on the wind,
the sweetness of air in my lungs.
To take my first sip of a frosty martini,
taste its citrus and juniper hints
beneath the iced burn on my tongue,
is to bless that exotic gray lump
for reminding me that I'm alive.

III. *Pieces of Time*

Making Our Mark

Like a high-ranking dog over-marking his rivals,
my husband pretended to cover with his own scent
each place I'd been with old boyfriends; afterward
nuzzling me like a cat rubbing its face against me
to make me its own. Scent-marking, it's called,
although seeing, for humans, is far more impactful
than sniffing: we need visible symbols to testify
to our presence in a particular place, at a particular time.
All those initials scratched on school desks, picnic
tables, wet cement—the same impulse that prompted
the crude pencil sketch on an inside wall of our farmhouse
(a man in a hat, cigarette dangling). And the bare butt-
prints, father and son, side by side on our hand-built
stone grill. It's ancient, this urge. Hohokam petroglyphs,
the fancy calligraphy of Spanish invaders, the block letters
of laborers building the railroads, along with graffiti
of current-day tourists: all carved in the sandstone
of El Morro Mesa. Consider the scenes from the film
"The Shawshank Redemption," the prisoner who chipped
Brooks was here just over the door frame from which
he hanged himself and where another man later added,
So was Red. From hand prints on the cave wall to spray-
painted tags on a boxcar, always these human voices:
We were here. We mattered. See us.

Object Lessons

Colors are the mother tongue of the subconscious. —Carl Jung

A revelation to me, when I saw the exhibit,
that those gleaming marble statues I love,
those bodies of perfect proportions, had once
been vividly painted—which led the exhibitors
to *paint replicas of the most famous in order to* show
they were not, as earlier scholars convinced us,
left purposefully bare by their creators
to heighten the glimmer of shadow and light
on pale skin.

A falsehood, that claim. Which compels me to ask,
why would artists who lived in countries awash
with the brilliance of sea and sky,
why would they leave their statues unpainted?
Why *not* clothe them in dizzying harlequin patterns,
as in this exhibit, or paint their skins olive,
their wounds dripping red?

Questions that lead me, as the curators intended,
to look askance at earlier scholars' dismissal
of traces of paint that still clung to the otherwise color-free
stone—as if whiteness reflected the purity of an ideal
in more than just bodies of marble. Questions
that also unsettle me when I admit that I feel overwhelmed
by this garish display. And chagrined to acknowledge
the pleasure I feel to remember the cool white marble
of those lovely sculptures, their power, even now,
to calm and unclutter my mind.

The Third Force

Pleasure and pain, like dissonant notes in a major-key chord,
exist side by side: a truth I glimpsed standing outside
the vet's when I gave myself over to weeping so deep
it felt good. Call it "sweet grief," that kind of pain,
as if a bodily wound were being washed clean. Red
flowers bloomed from the Virgin's tears as she gazed
on her crucified son—a reminder that beauty and sorrow,
like pleasure and pain, coexist, perhaps somehow
complete one another. I watched a friend break into tears
listening to Schubert's "Trout" quintet, recalled how my father,
during his last year of life, found music too lovely to bear,
felt united to both as I sobbed on the steps for the death of my cat.
As the Romans honored both beauty and war in the union
of Venus and Mars, so poppies spill out of derelict tanks
on the fields of the dead; so a blacksmith in eastern Ukraine
sculpts spent artillery shells and machine gun parts into roses:
each latter image a visual koan transcendent of logic.
How tender the balance between what we shrink from
and what we respond to in nature and art: the coral snake's
beauty, the burn of a spicy cuisine, *Guernica's* horror
confronted via the safety of canvas and paint.

Accidental Expressionism:
an Ekphrastic Poem

My artist friend finished the painting,
she said, with no meaning in mind, attention
focused only on textures, colors, and shapes.

Whereas I see a sunrise
over a purple-capped mountain,
gold splashing the dark sea below.

I see the first day of creation:
the primordial mound of the earth
heaved up, just a moment ago, from the deep.

I see the sun god Ra in the act of emergence,
his newborn glory reflected in gold
on the waters of chaos from which he arose.

That is, until a shift of perspective
(rather like closing one eye at a time
and changing the parallax angle)

changes the globe of the sun
into the cheek and blond head of a baby
asleep on the mountain surface: aslant,

belly down on its slope, an arm
and a leg hanging over the side
as if hugging an up-tilted mattress.

A work of art with a life of its own
despite what the artist intended
or the viewer expected to see.

What We See

A helmeted soldier in khaki, his dark eyes alert
above a camo-print mask, is framed by hollyhock spires
in the foreground, a woman behind him glancing away:
both ambiguous postures to the observer. Asked to count how often
a white-shirted team passed the ball, viewers failed to notice
the actor in a gorilla suit walking by. The "male gaze" means
looking at women as objects rather than persons; Victorians
kept their privies hidden away behind hollyhock fences
that also betrayed their location. In the Orpheus myth, one glance
dooms Eurydice to the Underworld forever. Goethe's Faust
sees a beautiful girl in the glass, an image that augurs her ruin.
Georgia O'Keeffe looked at flowers and saw there the intimate
contours of female bodies. My mother inspected her face
in the mirror for hours, noting each wrinkle and pore; I tried
to give myself dimples by clenching my cheeks in my teeth
as I drifted to sleep. In China, brass mirrors hung above idols
cause evil spirits to flee from their own reflections. The soldier
cradles his rifle, finger close to but not on the trigger; he neither
looks back at the woman nor at the hollyhocks wreathing his figure.

Where We Meet Again

for Jim

Last night you were with me once more
in the room of my dream:
sliding clean dishes into a cupboard,
closing a drawer in your desk,
shrugging into a plaid flannel shirt
as you moved toward the door.

Unaware of my surging emotion,
you neither ignored nor acknowledged my presence.
Your focus was elsewhere,
as often happened when I was reading
or you were driving: serenely assuming
the other would always be there.

I closed the distance between us
and clung to your arm
as if we were facing the wind.
All the while fighting tears
I could not let you see,
afraid of betraying my knowledge

of time—of *your* time—slipping away.

Purposeful Circumlocutions

I don't want to talk about trees.
Like my bountiful avocado, hurricane-blasted
down to a stump; or the clerodendrum
with leaves that flashed red in reverse;
or the skeletal pine snags beloved by birds—
those latter two bulldozed away by people
greedy for land. I don't want to speak
of the fine yellow maple whose canopy
buttered the light in my bedroom
each fall of my blithe middle age.

Nor am I inclined to talk about water—
not when it's formed into clouds shot through
with crepuscular rays like a picture-book Jesus—
and not in its liquid form, either.
Why speak about how it refreshes
a dry midnight mouth, or swaddles the body
in bathwater heat on a wintry day,
or creeps under snow-covered mittens,
chapping the wrists? Why bother to talk
about iron-tinged water tasting of blood,
or the time when Lake Michigan swallowed
and swallowed and swallowed a friend
until the lifeguard dove in? Why try to distinguish
water as currents that roil the rapids and crest into waves
from the pond water swirling with creatures
that shock school children?

Rather, I ask you to pay attention, to notice
what springs to your mind, then speak for yourself
about such things as water and trees.
These are yours, yours alone, to perceive.
Which will free me to sit here in silence,
looking back on my personal trees,
looking out through my window at Florida clouds,
looking inward to contemplate water—
that power that governs my zodiac sign,
that mutable element pulled by the moon into tides,
that sustainer of life and relentless dissolver—
in my own way.

How Misfortune Has Altered
My View of Misfortune

The live oak kinetic with squirrels,
the aloe plant cluster sprung
from a single spiked pup,
the clerodendrum grove's starburst blossoms,
the avocado tree heavy with fruit:
an invisible property line,
robbing me of the lush green expanse
I wrongly imagined my own,
has doomed it to fall to the bulldozer's blade.

I lie awake in the dark and lament my misfortune:
to be deprived of the land
from the back of my house
to the tangle of jungle enclosed by the fence
some previous tenant installed,
land that I made my own for ten years.
My long, peaceful solitude lost.
A third of my patio severed.
Merely a cramped strip of grass for my dogs.

*

The morning after Hurricane Ian,
I look out on a splintered scene:
a mocking mosaic by a tortured artist
that radically changes my view of misfortune.
I no longer mourn the live oak
that's cracked down the middle
and threatens to fall on the house.
No more regret at being deprived
of starburst trees now bent or snapped off,
an avocado uprooted past hope,

or the pines flung askance
beyond the section of chain-link
not ironed flat by the wind.
Empty of angst, I gaze at what's left,
grateful that others must cope with a mess
that's no longer my burden.

Only the aloes still stand, marking time.

Moments Lost

After Gerard Manley Hopkins

How to store—is there some, is there any such somewhere
To punch or push, to pulse or pluck sinew, no spark, sap, or spur
To shape the mind, save the past, to keep it from fading away?
Oh is there no slowing, no seal or staunch, for that dwindling
Down? No way to escape its slow fading or banish the elves of erasure—
Zealous elves, elves bold and eroding, bleaching all color away?
No, no one and nothing to keep the feel fresh,
Recover the daily, the doing, the detail,
Stamp a visage or voice, fix a feature in mind.
No way of undoing the dimming, of retaining the fever and force
Of a lost leitmotif, or tickle of snicker and quiver.
No hope of mooring the memories,
Of halting the raveling moments,
Of stopping the ball of nostalgia unspooling
To swaddle and stifle each delicate image
Within oblivion's gluey cocoon.
No, nothing, nothing to slow down the dance,
The dull disappearance, the final unwinding:
Forgetting, forgotten, foregone.

Her September Familiar

For Roxy

Now is the season when hummingbirds vanish,
daylight dwindles, and dying leaves fall,

a strange season of endings and losses,
colors fading to gray with a blackness behind.

A particular sorrow for her, this heartache,
even if shared by so many, akin to the sky grief we feel

at losing the stars, even the brightest invisible now
everywhere but the most rural night skies.

A more personal sorrow, too: the growing awareness
of how fragile her loved ones, family and friends,

this lingering grief for those absent, now or forever,
her people. As precious and ever-present as the invisible stars,

as essential to her as signal fires in a storm,
when everything seems, everything *is,* so precarious.

Each year it comes, this melancholy, her familiar,
not with the surprise of a window thrown suddenly open

to weather but as her September companion.
Until one day, down the road, it departs to the rattling call

of sandhill cranes overhead, a flurry of cedar waxwings,
and a pair of fawns still dressed in their white polka dots.

To the Season of Spring Returning

After Gerard Manley Hopkins

Spring begins now; now, egregious in green, the stalks rise
From their graves; around me, what tree-tricks! what clusters
Of catkins illumine the willows! has a wilder willful-waxing
Of yellow dust buttered ever and brightened the skies?

I gaze, I breathe in, I wend
Though the ambient freshness of soil to seize the ephemera
Of may apple parasols, leaf-litter-sprung and unfurled,
And the bird-beaks of unopened tulips before their dear petals unbend.

Such fecundity, birthed from, made out of a body
Bountiful ever—red-lipped-fruitful Lakshmi!—
These things, these things still return despite shoddy
Defacings; so that, when springtime reaches its acme,
She will bloom, lotus-lush, in water translucent or cloudy
And run riot, rampaging in richness enough to distract me.

Renewal

At first I mistake it for the burr
of a faraway phone: the rat-a-tat-tat
of the woodpecker's beak,
its jackhammer head a red blur
as it skitters along the wood beam
of the shade-cloth stretched over my flowers.
Then both of us, drummer and watcher,
equally startled by a swoop from above.
A plunging gray missile strafing the grass,
semaphoring a warning in mockingbird code:
the flashing of under-wing white
as it soars upward again—
You're too close to my nest!

Well, of course: it is spring. A friend,
widowed four years and now newly in love,
radiates joy in a full-body aura that lights up
the room. Next to the glow of her sun,
my own contentment's a day-moon
made of morning birdsong and bustle:
a renewal that feels as fortuitous
as the star-sapphire ring I lost decades ago
and found in the lining of an old coat.

No new loves or do-overs for me.
With this exception, improved hearing aids:
a fresh patch of pleasure that brims like a pool
with the jovial hubbub of birds.

Acknowledgments

"Almost Bionic," *Mosaic Art & Literary Journal*, Edition 61, 2022.

"*Danse de l'arboriste*," *Superpresent*, March/April 2023.

"The Sisters Corner," *Freshwater Literary Journal*, Spring 2023.

"The Intimate Room," *Halfway Down the Stairs*, June 1, 2023.

"How Misfortune Altered My View of Misfortune," *Hamilton Stone Review*, #48, Spring 2023.

"Moments Lost," *Lothlorien Poetry Journal*, August 9, 2023 (published as "Hiraeth").

"Burning Mouth Syndrome," *Lothlorien Poetry Journal*, August 9, 2023.

"Accidental Expressionism," *Lothlorien Poetry Journal*, August 9, 2023.

"Where We Meet Again," *Toasted Cheese Literary Journal*, #23:3, September 2023.

"Seeing Stars," *Burningword Literary Journal*, Issue 108, October 2023.

"Tongues in Trees," *The Wise Owl*, November 2023.

"Apex Predators," *Freshwater Literary Journal*, Winter 2023.

"What We See," *Cerasus*, Issue 11, Winter 2024.

"Her September Familiar, *The Lake*, January 2024.

"Making Our Mark," *Superpresent*, Spring 2024.

"Loving the Questions," *Superpresent*, Spring 2024.

"No Power in a Square, *The Lake*, May 2024.

"The Third Force, *Orchards Poetry Journal*, Summer 2024.

"Litmus in the Lunchbox," *The Wise Owl*, July 2024.

"A Tumor Made of Teeth Found in the Pelvis of an Ancient Egyptian," *TwinBird Review*, Issue 2.1, Summer 2024.

"Rites of Passage, *The Basilisk Tree*, September 2024.

"Missing Pieces," *Amsterdam Quarterly*, March 2024; *AQ 2024 Yearbook*, December 2024.

"On the Dance Floor with Glass," *Abstract: Contemporary Expressions*, forthcoming September 2025.

"In A Family Way, *Abstract: Contemporary Expressions*, forthcoming September 2025.

Title Index

First Line Index

www.ingramcontent.com/pod-product-compliance
Lightning Source LLC
Chambersburg PA
CBHW010042090426
42734CB00019B/3253